Kellie o'Dempsey

Tossed in the air by the Fates,
a single rose
pivots and turns on its descent
towards the front-row seat
of this once-in-a-lifetime performance.

The fresh bloom falls
as a young daughter enters
the theatre of induction.

The death of a mother.

Too soon, the performance has begun …

"I don't think any of us can deny our experiences even if we do lock them away. They still influence us ..."

— Margaret

"I feel so cheated because I did not get to know my mom as a friend versus just my mom …"

— Sarah

Praise for The Girls in the Front Row

"As a motherless daughter (and mother of daughters), I read with a sense of recognition, connection and appreciation. The daughters' stories continue to resonate because, while deeply felt, they are unsentimental; therein lies their power. Linda Gayle Ross encourages readers to understand and to share their own stories, forging a connection with her audience that is powerful and deserved.

Deeply moving ... important ... beautiful composition ... remarkable photographs and artwork."

— Donna Walsh Inglehart, author of *Breaking the Ring*, the critically-acclaimed Civil War novel *Grindstone,* and co-author (with Ian Coristine, best-selling author and photographer) of *One in a Thousand*

"Stunning ... clean ... powerful ... brilliant ... stops you in your tracks."

— Kathryn Wood, National Capital Resources Inc.

The Girls in the Front Row

EXPLORING THE IMPACT OF LOSING A MOTHER YOUNG
Stories. Secrets. Lessons.

LINDA GAYLE ROSS

This edition published in Canada by PrairieCORE Ltd.
Printed and bound in Canada.

The Girls in the Front Row © 2012 by Linda Gayle Ross
ISBN 978-0-9879460-0-3
A record for this book can be found on legal deposit with Library and Archives Canada.

For information about special discounts on bulk purchases for education or non-profits, please contact info@prairiecore.com.

Creative and art direction, design and production by SmallWorld Marketing Group *www.swmg.ca*
Principal photography by Suzy Lamont
Original art by Kellie O'Dempsey
Printed by C.J. Graphics Inc., Printers & Lithographers
134 Park Lawn Road, Toronto, Canada M8Y 3H9

Contents

Acknowledgments

For me, original work results from creative conversation.

My thanks to Alyson Charette, Citizen Harcourt, Heidi and Suzy Lamont, Sharon Monson, Pamela Orser, Dena Paxton, Donna Rutherford and Rena Upitis for your input at an early focus group.

To Suzy Lamont for helping me prepare for this session and to Citizen Harcourt for researching the scope of early mother loss.

To Tracy Carson, Rickardo Giuliani, Todd Morgan, Laurie Ross, Rob Wood, Stephen Wild and

Deb Hamilton — thank you for your talents and inspiration.

To Deanna Knight for always asking, always caring.

To Madam Justice Anne C. Trousdale for your wise counsel on families and what matters.

Thank you to the Grand Theatre in Kingston, Canada and the Thousand Islands Playhouse in Gananoque, Canada for sharing your space for photo shoots.

To Dr. Rena Upitis for your wise counsel, friendship

and generosity. My thanks for taking The Girls through a guided facilitation session. You are a wonder.

To Joan Sherman for your friendship, communications savvy and certainty that I could get this right.

To Kellie O'Dempsey whose creative energy and rare talent knock my socks off. We are oceans apart but I feel your ongoing support. Thank you, Kellie o, for embracing me and this project.

To my friend Ian Coristine who always encourages me to sweat the details.

And to my family, my step-children, all of you, thank you. I know at times you've wondered.

To my sister, Maureen, Warrior Woman, for your courage. And to my daughter, Dorie, my heartbeat. Before Dora died she made an angel promise that one day you'd arrive.

And finally, to my husband, Doug. Life with you is an adventure. Thank you for believing in me and for making me laugh each and every day.

Creative Team

Suzy Lamont is the award-winning principal photographer for *The Girls in the Front Row*. Her images have been featured widely, most recently in *Grace Ormonde Wedding Style*, *GLASS Quarterly* and *New Glass*.

Suzy became a Front Row Girl at the age of twenty-five. When asked to lend her creativity to *The Girls*, her eyes filled with tears, saying, "love to ... I feel as if a bouquet has just popped out of my chest." Suzy created *Mum in Ice* (see far left photo below) soon after in response to my nostalgic comment, "my mother is frozen in time." Such are her creative instincts.

Suzy's message for Front Row Girls everywhere: Be present.

Suzy Lady, my sincere thanks for your unwavering commitment to *The Girls*. To the journey. And for your talent, patience, good humour, wisdom and indulgence.

Small World Marketing Group (SWMG) brands communities through strategy, creative and communications enabling magic and opportunity for clients in Canada, USA and abroad.

Tracy John, co-owner and creative director of SWMG, is an artistic genius, a print designer extraordinaire, an emerging Canadian designer in unique fused glass and a Front Row Girl. As Creative Director for *The Girls*, Tracy lent her expertise in editorial design and advertising.

Karen Labern's commitment to *The Girls* is everywhere in these pages. Under Tracy's direction, she took the lead on many of the unique design elements and approaches. She's a talented young designer and terrific team member to work with. Karen, you rock.

Steven Sheffield has an amazing eye for detail. Printing presses, colour correction, cameras and scanners are in his DNA. No image leaves SWMG without his trained eye upon it. Steven's translation from image to print is exceptional.

My heartfelt thanks to Tracy, Karen and Steven for knowing that the powerful and inspiring stories of the *The Girls in the Front Row* must be viewed through a design lens of colour, clarity and pizazz.

Deborah Melman-Clement is a talented and versatile writer with communications expertise in all of its many forms. As editor, she questioned, queried and nudged me gently forward. Thank you, Mrs., for sticking close and sharing some of the best/worst winter weekends ever.

Photos by Stephen Wild

To the Girls in the Front Row

For your courage, your wisdom, your laughter, your tears.

For being scared to tell your stories but allowing me to tell them anyway.

For your gift of hope to motherless daughters everywhere.

To my mother

Dora Patience Ross

I am YOU.

Introduction

We were all between nine and twenty-nine when we each claimed a front-row seat in the theatre of induction, our mother's early death.

Now we are between the ages of sixteen and ninety.

In the late 1990s, I discovered Hope Edelson's ground-breaking book, *Motherless Daughters*, and found myself in the first few pages. I recall being on an airplane, her book in my lap, when the young blond woman seated next to me smiled and said, "You too?" For the remainder of that flight we talked about our shared experiences of shame and loneliness, our families that had changed forever after our mothers died, rituals that stopped and other women who stole our fathers' time and resources while seeming not to notice or care how much we still needed him.

The thing is, if you are a motherless daughter, a Front Row Girl, you don't often discover that someone seated next to you by chance understands your insides so well because hers feel the same.

I would continue to read more about early mother loss from time to time and wonder about its impact on my life, but in 2008 it was time for me to try to understand more. I recruited a small group of Girls to explore this experience with, and this thing called "closure." By then I knew for certain that grief refuses to follow a prescribed path.

My goal was to capture true stories of motherless daughters now at all ages and surround them with visuals. As facts alone rarely inspire, I hoped this approach would connect others to the experience, making it easier to "see" and understand.

Creating this work has had a profound impact on me.

As I asked others to share their stories, I knew that I would need to do the same. I am grateful for this, as I've discovered that in the telling, the burden has become lighter.

In *The Girls in the Front Row*, you will come face to face with sorrow and triumph.

We have secrets. Some are spoken here, others not yet.

One Front Row Girl shared her story with me on the condition that her name remain confidential. For her, sadness became determination. She is now a remarkable woman and a professional superstar. Danielle (not her name) was twenty-four when her mother died. Danielle's mother was young when she was diagnosed and later institutionalized with Alzheimer's Disease. She spent her last years in a chair, rocking and moaning, with no ability to communicate with anyone.

Danielle and her two siblings grew up largely fending for themselves. Their father had begun a relationship with the teenager next door while Danielle's mother was still at home and well enough to chastise him for his behaviour. When she died, Danielle's father married this young woman and moved her into the family home. Collapsing in tears one day, Danielle found many of her mother's special things in a garbage bag at the front curb.

Thankfully, their mother's sister, Aunt Matilda, watched over them as they grew, helping to provide them with a sense of home and family. She overrode many of their father's commands with her customary spunk. Aunt Matilda made sure birthdays were remembered, rituals happened and Christmases were celebrated. She helped with schooling and, in part due to her influence, each child went on to higher education. Collectively "the kids" are now successful entrepreneurs and high-powered executives. Two work internationally, in English as well as other languages. And they remain connected to each other, sharing holidays, families and lives.

Sadness, anger and bitterness from their childhood experiences remain. As Danielle reminds me, "this work is about the journey, not the end. We're all still on it."

There's at least one major lesson from Danielle's story: Reach out and find your Aunt Matilda.

My older sister, Maureen, and I have often joked that while I am a Front Row Girl, she is not. It's not clear to either of us why. While she may not consider herself a Front Row Girl, she has truly become a Warrior Woman.

In June of 2011, Maureen's husband of over thirty years shot himself in the head in front of her. It would take days for her to close her eyes, and months before she would experience a few short hours of uninterrupted sleep.

So many aspects of this tragic event reminded me of the need to publish *The Girls in the Front Row*, true stories that might help to inspire others. Death scares, sometimes terrifies, often leaving those most affected in silence, loneliness, denial and unresolved grief.

I have now met post-traumatic stress and its companions, anger, grief and guilt.

But my sister and I are no strangers to death. We both knew that she would need to give those who had known their family for years and were in shock and disbelief "permission" to speak to her. We broke the silence by creating a message for her Facebook page and a short article for her local newspaper. Emails and supportive calls started arriving and hugs happened now at chance meetings in her small town.

Maureen has had the courage to reach out and stay connected to others as she re-imagines her future and moves from darkness to light.

I smile that she does not think of herself as a Front Row Girl. I think that she has jumped to front row, centre.

While life will have its way with us — big disappointments, sudden deaths, unspeakable tragedies — I'm learning that we must have the courage to reach out for help as we struggle into the new skin we'll need to move forward.

The first interview question I asked each Front Row Girl was, "Please tell me about the day your mother died. Where was she? Where were you? What do you remember most about that day?"

While there were many tears shed in recalling "that day", this question became a gift. As Carolyn (page 55) reminds me, "no one ever asks you to talk about the day your mom died and that's really sad. Maybe a therapist might, but nobody that matters, like your friends or family."

As you read the stories of *The Girls in the Front Row*, maybe you will think of someone you know, especially someone you love, that longs to be asked that question. If you ask, and can be prepared for any answer, you will be remembered forever.

Meet the Girls in the Front Row

It took from April, 2008 to October, 2011 to find The Girls.

I wanted to talk with a small group of women who had all lost their moms before they were thirty. While many significant life events like education, marriage, career challenges and babies begin before thirty, most remain unfinished.

There were so many questions that I wanted to explore: When your mother dies young, who is there to help you choose your graduation gown, your wedding gown? Who helps you through the rough patches? What happens on holidays? Who remembers birthdays and helps you celebrate rites of passage? What if you don't have an Aunt Matilda or a mother figure? Who is there to say, "I am proud of you?"

My guiding principle was "do no harm." I was comfortable interviewing women who'd been without their mothers for years, like me, but unsure about involving Girls, both young and new to this seminal life event.

I had recently met Maegan (page 27) and we were in a restaurant, chatting one day. She was then twenty-two and about to graduate from a prominent university. Her father had already been dead for years, her

mother had died a few short years earlier and as a result, Maegan now had custody of her half-sister, Emma. At one point Maegan stopped talking and looked at me with tears in her eyes, saying, "I just want to meet someone who's ninety who will tell me if this will ever stop." Maegan and Emma became Front Row Girls soon after. And Maegan did meet a ninety-year-old, another Front Row Girl, Gwen (page 71), whose energy and wisdom inspired her and helped the rest of us understand how it can get easier, softer, closer to stopping.

The Girls are Canadian, American and Australian. They are bright, creative, courageous and resourceful. One is in high school and headed for university, two are community college graduates. Others are university graduates at the undergraduate, Masters and PhD levels. They are single, single moms, married with children and stepchildren and married with grown children and grandchildren.

They will help you understand the impact of losing a mother young. You may shed tears as you read their stories, but I am certain that you will admire their courage and commitment. Their pluck. They have all moved forward with their mothers tucked tightly in their hearts.

Mine is the final story. All of our stories are true.

The Approach

After many conversations between photographer Suzy Lamont and me, a small informal focus group and several middle-of-the night musings, it was time to begin.

All of the interviews were audiotaped. They occurred in my office, in private restaurant booths, at my home, by telephone and via Skype. I asked sixteen questions through which The Girls told me their stories. All wanted to talk, to try to understand more, to help others. Most cried. One acknowledged that it had taken her so long to agree to be part of this project because she had cried so much when her mother died years earlier that she couldn't face the thought of more tears. Some made me promise to keep their secrets while others thought it was now time to talk.

I love to interview and I've been told that I'm good at it, but these interviews were the most difficult I've ever done. After some of the sessions I retreated to the safety of my bed and quilt, but most of the tears I shed there were in awe of the sorrow, courage and triumph I heard portrayed.

My first interview was in a private booth in a restaurant with Shirley Towriss Ross (page 67). We drank tea, laughed and cried as I heard the story of her

mother's sudden, tragic death more than fifty years earlier, facts and feelings rarely spoken of before.

Meetings, emails and phone conversations offered further insights as I met others who would become Front Row Girls.

In the fall of 2009 I brought The Girls together for a day, requesting that each bring a special object that had belonged to their mothers. Some had no memorabilia, as their

mothers' possessions had been callously disposed of years earlier by another. However, with her customary creative energy, Suzy Lamont captured (with or without mementos) many of the images in this book that day.

In the fall of 2010, with The Girls now a larger group, we met again to take a deeper look at the impact of early mother loss. Dr. Rena Upitis generously shared her time and energy to facilitate a session

Kellie o'Dempsey

that led us across the timeline of our lives to capture some of our experiences of sorrow and triumph. Now we had many eyes and hearts at work at once.

Suzy took more photographs of The Girls that day. She also caught most of the theatre shots appearing in *The Girls in the Front Row*, all taken at the Grand Theatre in Kingston, Canada.

My final interview was conducted on November 12, 2011 via Skype with Australian artist Kellie O'Dempsey (page 47). I asked the same sixteen questions, and from across the world I heard the now-familiar themes of abandonment, denial, silence, loneliness and shame. And I heard more stunning insights and examples of courage and triumph. Kellie and I also discovered that, while oceans apart, we share both the experience of early mother loss and the same names of close family members. Maurice, her uncle and my late father, and Maureen, our sisters — hers younger, mine older.

Suzy's images of Kellie were also captured via Skype (page 49). We had found a way to interview and photograph a Front Row Girl on the other side of the world.

With hours of interviews, emails, conversations and group sessions complete, it was time to tell our stories.

the playful
Ferru according to Gombrich, may ha
the similar scene described by Lucian
XV of Alexander and Roxana. Tietze-Conrat
on Magazine, XLVII, 1925) has noted that th
osition of the figures reclining in oppos

The Girls in the Front Row

Hearts will never be practical until they are made unbreakable ...
The Wizard of Oz

Our **Stories**

The person I was so emotionally attached to

was my mom.

Me: 11 Mom: 44

Emma Maingot, Canada

I don't know if I was actually feeling sick that morning or if I was just feeling down, but I begged my stepdad not to go to school and so I was there when she died.

Looking back, I feel like I should have been a lot more shocked, but I guess I knew it was coming. I didn't cry. I know that I was quiet the whole day. I don't remember what I was thinking. I feel like I wasn't thinking very much. I wish that I could remember more, but I just can't.

I never liked crying in front of everyone so if I was going to do it, I would be by myself. I've been told that I keep

My friends do ordinary things — like talking to their moms.

I can't do that.

my emotions bottled up, but I don't try to. My sister, Maegan, said that before Mom died I was really cuddly and emotional, and after I changed. But I think that was because the person I was so emotionally attached to was my mom.

Mom's death has definitely made Maegan mature faster. When we were living together and she was in university, it kind of took away her youth because she couldn't go out and party. She had to be so careful what she did so that I was able to live with her and not be judged by society. At the time a lot of my friends' parents thought that she wasn't capable of being my guardian, but if they knew her, they'd have understood that she's like ten times more responsible than any parent because she had to be.

I know that Maegan became more like a parent than a friend or sibling because we used to fight and hurt each other.

I developed this whole new respect for her when we were living together, as she had to learn to treat me differently too, because as a sibling there was always my mom to separate us if we got out of hand.

My friends do ordinary things like talking to their moms. I can't do that. Some of their disrespect for both of their parents really bothers me. You'd think that in front of me they would respect their mothers a little more because they know that I know how lucky they really are.

I've definitely had moments where I am literally emotionally touched by what some of my friends' moms do for me in a motherly way because I don't have that.

I've been rowing competitively for my school. My mom used to do that. And Maegan rides and my mom used to do that, so we feel connected to her in that way.

Ever since Maegan went away to grad school I have been back living with our stepfather. It was a big decision for her to leave me here so I could stay in my school. I don't know what I'd do if he wasn't here for me. I've never lived with my own dad.

The best way to feel connected to my mom is to talk about her a lot, share memories, remember funny stories. We have pictures everywhere in the house. I know some people are surprised that we mention her so much. It's a sad subject, but it doesn't have to be so depressing. You should remember her partly in a happy way because she was living at one time and those were happy, happy times.

I don't know what's next for me, but I do know I can always count on Maegan.

The best way to feel connected to my mom is to talk about her a lot, share memories, remember funny stories. We have pictures everywhere in the house.

It was odd because I was comforted that Mom and Dad were finally together. It was like she had somewhere to go.

Me: 18 Mom: 44

Maegan McConnell, Canada

I was eleven when Mom was diagnosed with breast cancer. I'd already lost my father. He was a helicopter pilot and he died in a crash on January 28, 1988. I never met him. I was born on his birthday, August 12. Captain Daniel Mark McConnell would have turned twenty-seven that day.

Mom died at home on February 16, 2007. I was eighteen and at university nearby.

My stepfather, Ed, and my sister, Emma, and I were on her bed with her. I remember sitting beside her and praying to my father to take her away because she wasn't there anymore and she was in pain and suffering. And literally as soon as that thought went through my mind, it was done.

It was odd because I was comforted that Mom and Dad were finally together. It was like she had somewhere to go. The worst thing is that you feel relief. It had been

years and years of worrying and being stressed and pretending that you're fine.

My mother was my best friend. She was my idol. She was everything. We rode horses together. I spent all kinds of time with her and so did my friends.

I don't remember much of the next few months, but I didn't drop out of university. I went back to class the next week. I needed to stay in control and I wanted my mother to be proud of me. I remember being at the gym and looking around, thinking, "My mom died last week and nobody knows." That's the weird thing: Your world changes forever and everyone else's seems to just keep going.

I don't let a lot of people into my world. I didn't really before, but it's even less now. The most important people in my life, my parents, are no longer here, so

why would I think anybody else would stick around? At the same time I do know that I have fabulous support— Emma, my grandparents, Ed, my friends, tons.

I had custody of Emma three days before Mom died. We moved in together when she went into Grade Nine and while I finished my undergraduate degree. I am a sister/mom and it's pretty strange at times, but we're making it through. Since I've been away at graduate school, Emma has been living with Ed. He's being wonderful. I was pretty hard on him when Mom died. It took me about three years to realize that his wife died too, not just my mother. I've also gotten used to the fact that he needs to move on in his life too.

I've always told Emma this isn't meant to break us. I remember seeing a TV show with a little girl beside her

dying mom and her father saying, "Think of it this way, the two worst things that are ever going to happen to you just did." So now at times I remember this and I think, 'Okay, we can do this. Yes, we can do this.'

I believe all of this has brought out that I need to always be in control. I don't like surprises. I wasn't like this before because I was so dependent on my mom. I always wanted her to be in control.

Mom had Emma because she wanted me to have a sibling in case anything happened to her. Well, it did. That's why I'll never have an only child. If anything ever happens, I need to know that there's somebody else.

Okay, we can do this.
Yes, we can do this.

Whenever I catch a scent of her perfume, I think of her and she fills my heart.

Me: 16 Mom: 51

Becky Gale, Canada

I look at my dad sometimes and I wonder how he does it because he lost both his wife and his son. I love him and I want to be just like him. He's a role model for me.

My dad ran into my room at 5:13 in the morning. He was on the phone to 911. He said, "I think Mom's having a heart attack." I ran over to the bathroom and knelt beside her. She'd been getting radiation for lung cancer and that morning she'd started coughing and her lungs had filled with blood. It ended up everywhere. Two ambulances, a fire truck and four cop cars showed up.

At the hospital, I remember both my dad and my brother crying. I was in such shock, I couldn't cry. Afterwards we drove home and I helped my dad clean the blood out of the bathroom.

I remember just sitting and crying.

Mom died on May 29, 2006, three days after she turned fifty-one.

She died on a Monday and I went back to school that Wednesday because I needed to get back to band and sports. I just couldn't stay in the house anymore. When I got there all the kids were like, "I'm so sorry, blah, blah, blah." I know they were just being nice, but it was not what I wanted to hear. I had one friend that was great though. When he found out, he didn't say anything. He just gave me the biggest hug ever, and that's what I needed. Just to feel understood and loved.

I was the one who found out that Mom had breast cancer in 2000. She didn't tell my dad, she didn't tell my brother. I was there when she went for blood tests. I remember just sitting and crying. But we weren't a family that talked. My mom was so much fun and she was was always there for us,   but we never talked about anything — ever.

My mother smelled so good. Whenever I catch a scent of her perfume, I think of her and she fills my heart.

Before Mom passed away, Dad and I didn't talk much. He travelled so much for his work. We've learned how to talk more now and this is   making such a difference.

Two years after Mom died, my brother committed suicide. I have never felt that kind of pain in my life. It felt like an elephant stepped on my chest. I look at my dad sometimes and I wonder how he does it because he lost both his wife and his son. I love him and I want to be just like him. He's a role model for me. He's done much more grief work than I have and I think he's amazing.

Dad had another woman in his life after Mom died. He waited before dating her. I've had trouble accepting her, but I know that she helped him so much when he needed it and I respect this. It's not really that I resented her in my mom's place, it's just that I couldn't wrap my head around the whole thing. It's been hard on us all.

After Mom died, I developed a drinking problem — a bad coping mechanism — but I'm working on this. I'm fixing it.

Losing my mother has had a huge impact on my life. My friendships were really good before Mom passed away. Afterward it felt like everyone just kind of left me in the dark. My relationships would be better now, but because of what has happened I have a hard time trusting. And what about my brother? Would he still be alive if Mom were here?

Thursday, May 27/82

Dear mom,

Hope this letter reaches you

@ be in London. I still don't know who'll be with me. Probably just Rainbow though.

Sue's water basically broke a couple of hours ago. She's doing fine. You will have received a cable way before now announcing the baby's birth. Should happen within the next 48 hours.

I've been reading "A Guide to Midwifery" since I got there. I didn't want to tell you this before cause you may have panicked thinking I would be doing the actual delivery. Ernie will be doing the delivery and I will be assisting him and coaching Sue. I do believe I'll really get into this though. I'm thinking I might do some studying on it and maybe midwife in the townships. They usually work in pairs. I really think ...thing can be ideal ...self-conscio...

Me: 9 Mom: 35

Carly Griffith, Canada

There's something instinctual, something innate, that a mother and child have together.

I'm a midwife, and I found a letter my mom wrote to her mom forever ago talking about how she'd like to be a midwife. So strange. Did I know this somehow?

I think about my mom a lot when "my babies" are being born because a lot of women have their moms with them during birth and postpartum. I also think about how I'll miss her when that happens for me.

It was July 15, 1993, just ten days short of her thirty-sixth birthday and on her wedding anniversary — but not to my dad. I was at my father's family's cottage with him,

I remember missing
my mom like crazy,
but it wasn't because

I didn't feel supported
or loved or safe.

my uncle and my cousin.
My cousin and I were doing
watercolour in the dining room
when my dad came in, sat next
to me and said, "Your mom's
suffering is over."

I remember this very distinctly.
I absolutely knew what it meant.
My dad had explained that
she wasn't going to get better
months prior to that. It started
out as breast cancer, but then it
became everything cancer. Both
of us started crying. I was only
nine, but I can picture where I
was sitting, where he was sitting,
where my cousin was sitting. I
can see the light in the room.

My mom died at my
grandparents' home. She
had a night nurse, but my
grandmother looked after her
during the day. Mom had a hospital bed and an IV with pain
medication all of the time.

After she died I moved back to
Toronto with my father.

It was hard being without my
family, my brother, my friends.
I went on to make my life in
Ontario, but I continue to go
back to Quebec as often as I can
every year to see my family.
I miss them.

Dad had a hard time losing
my mom, even though they
weren't together. He has
wrestled with an alcohol
addiction for many years that
has caused him and all of us
who love him great pain.

Joy, my stepmom, had to
be strong for me. She knew
she was now the maternal role in
my life, as much as I resisted that
sometimes. I remember missing
my mom like crazy, but it wasn't
because I didn't feel supported
or loved or safe. Joy has been a
role model for me. She has
created opportunities for me
that I am very grateful for.

As much as I love Joy and
we get along great, I don't

think it's ever the same kind of relationship. There's something instinctual, something innate that a mother and child have together. Still, my grandmother has told me that my mom told her she was happy that I had Joy. Mom felt reassured leaving me with Joy and that makes me feel good too.

My grandmother, my mom's mom, is really important to me. She's the closet connection I have to my mother biologically and personally. We sit and talk about my mom a lot.

I think the best thing to do if you lose your mom when you're a kid is to ask people to tell you stories. Hearing others' experiences of her is priceless to me, as my experiences are limited. Years ago I had someone say "your mom gave the best hugs." Wow. I've emailed people and asked them for their stories. I've learned so much about her that way.

It did give me peace to be able to tell her to go.
I loved my mom so much.

Me: 17 Mom: 44

Sarah Thompson, Canada

I feel so cheated because I did not get to know my mom as a friend versus just my mom.

It happened at night — November 24, 1996. I was cuddling with her and I remember closing my hands on hers and telling her how much I loved her and that she needed to go. The cancer was everywhere. I wanted her to stop suffering.

It did give me peace to be able to tell her to go. I loved my mom so much. My parents adopted me when I was a baby and I've always felt very special being their daughter.

They were high school sweethearts.

I am so happy that out of all that pain came such joy.

There were lots of people at the hospital, but the thing I remember most about that day was that my dad showed up and I was so upset. My parents had separated about a year earlier. Mom said she left him because he was cheating on her.

My best friend, Melissa, came home with me that night. We made a big fire and just talked and cried all night.

A couple of years later, when Dad and I finally talked and we'd become closer again, he told me that he had never cheated on Mom. He said she was taking medications for her illness that were making her delusional. He'd done lots of research on the medications. Dad said that, in the end, he made the choice to give me to my mom so I could be there for her when she needed me and just give her all my love. He said Mom had become paranoid and she wouldn't listen to him. She'd broken his heart.

I kept the house my mom and I lived in and stayed there for my last year of high school, although I wasn't at school much. I had a good group of girlfriends and they became my family to open up to. Somehow they'd know when I needed a girls' night and they'd slide over to my house and we'd sit around, watch a movie, light a fire, stuff like that. I don't think they'll ever understand what they did for me.

I was so lucky that I wasn't forced to do something I wasn't ready to do. It helped. I needed to be in the house with Mom's things and our things, to say goodbye.

Then it was time. After a few months I realized that I was staying there just to have a connection with Mom and I needed to let go. I sold the house and moved in with Dad and my stepmother. I needed a family again. I was having some emotional struggles and I needed their support. I am so happy that out of all of that pain came such joy. I reconnected with my dad and I do feel like I have

having kids triggered it.

Now each year in the weeks leading up to the anniversary of my mother's death, I'll be a little more sensitive, a little more introverted. I'm just missing her. I know it won't ever end. I feel so cheated

I was so lucky because I wasn't forced to do something that I wasn't ready to do. It helped. I needed to be in the house with Mom's things and our things, to say goodbye.

the best stepmother in the world.

During the first five years after my mother's death, I would miss her all the time. A movie would trigger it. A parent with her daughter on the street would trigger it. Thinking about

that I did not get to know my mom as a friend versus just my mom.

I have a beautiful little girl now and I'm so looking forward to passing along my mom's values and morals to her. Just everything.

It felt like my friends' lives just kept going on while *mine had changed forever.*

Me: 13 Mom: 47

Kirsten Knipp, USA

Independence and control are huge for me;
I made sure that I got a good education.

It was a Sunday night, April 1, 1989. I wanted to go to the mall but I had to do a bunch of chores before Mom would let me go. I was acting like a defiant thirteen-year-old. The last thing that happened before I left for the mall was that we were yelling at each other — still one of my most vivid memories of that day.

She didn't come home that night, but we didn't find out she was dead until Wednesday.

At the time, my parents were in the process of splitting up. Mom had gone out that evening to a church support

I have girlfriends with really strong relationships with their moms and I

don't get who this person is that they talk to and what it is they talk about.

group to help her deal with the pending divorce and cancer diagnosis she had recently received. Based on police reports, we believe that she had gone walking by a lake in one of the nearby neighbourhoods with a beautiful trail, had suffered a contusion to her head and drowned.

Everything changed after that. My brother and I were devastated. We had a lot of anger toward my dad. We needed his support, but we were so angry and there was a lot of confusion and silence. I do believe that Dad tried to help in his own way, but this new situation was nothing like his usual role with us. He'd always worked a lot, sometimes locally and sometimes in other cities.

I'm sure my father must have felt torn because he was determined to continue his life and maintain a personal relationship with a new woman.

She moved in with us and they got married about a year later. I finally just decided to get over my anger. She didn't try to be a mother figure, mostly she tried to be my friend.

A lot of my friendships became strained and I remember not knowing what to talk about. It felt like my friends' lives just kept on going while mine had changed forever.

Independence and control are huge for me; I made sure that I got a good education.

I feel saddest about losing my mom when there is a big milestone in my life — graduating from college, if I ever get married. I feel cheated that I don't get to share those moments. During times of serious emotional pain, when you just want to go to somebody and cry, I really miss her. I've mostly learned how to suppress this.

I have girlfriends with really strong relationships with their moms and I don't get who this person is that they talk to all the time and what it is they talk about. What helped for me was finding friends and learning to rely on them for emotional support. Once I was in my late twenties I realized that my

that I didn't have the support network others have? Was I ashamed that I couldn't fend for myself? It's hard to figure out what the shame was about.

Here's what I've learned: No one but you looks out for you no matter what promises are made, so you absolutely have to take

I used to be ashamed to ask for or accept help. Was I ashamed my mother died? Was I ashamed that I didn't have the support network others have? Was I ashamed that I couldn't fend for myself? It's hard to figure out what the shame was about.

girlfriends were very important in terms of insights.

I used to be ashamed to ask for or accept help. Was I ashamed my mother died? Was I ashamed

care of yourself. Hopefully you can find someone to partner with on that but, as they say, hope is not a strategy. While you look out for you, the best advice I can give is to reach out and ask for help.

Through my performance art
I explore aspects of experience in a public way.

Me: 14 Mum: 44

Kellie O'Dempsey, Australia

Under the mountain of flowers you could just see the edge of a coffin.

The hearse remained stationary. It would not move.
I remember my sister screaming for the car to drive on. To just go.
It seemed to stay forever. I couldn't understand why.

She howled.

Excerpt from "The Procession" by Kellie O'Dempsey

At university, my wonderful mentor, Art Mother Glenys, found me and saw me through it all. She still does.

My little sister Maureen was screaming. It sounded like a greyhound running across the car park to the cricket oval near the pub and straight across to the heat of the day.

Uncle Morris took us outside to tell us Mum was dead.

Maureen ran inside to Dad. "We just have to keep working," he told her. She went to the pub's wash house and ironed every piece of cloth there. I went across the road to the jetty and sat underneath where the shore met the water. I am sure I howled.

I know I smoked a lot of cigarettes.

We owned the Paynesville Pub, and Dad and my brother and sister were somewhere inside. Mum had tried it all — western and Chinese medicine, spirituality, religious inspiration. But when she knew she was dying it was, "Okay, it's time." She made us all promise to stay friends and left each of us envelopes containing poems and prayers. Her handwriting still makes me stir.

The funeral was weird. Our little town just shut its doors and everyone formed a massive motorcade to the cemetery. My dad, my older sister and my brother were part of this closing of the earth to my mom, but Maureen and I weren't. Mum's decision.

It felt strange walking through town knowing that everyone knew our business. At school my friends didn't mention it. The loneliness was huge. I remember the feelings, but not the details. I developed a huge fantasy life. Owning a pub, we had access to a lot of space, cigarettes, booze.

We didn't talk about it. We didn't talk about anything.

Afterward, Maureen and I were sent to an all-girls boarding school in the city run by the Presentation Sisters, a Catholic order dedicated to women's education. It was here I focused on my creative side. I was not the most disciplined student, and I spent all my time in the art room. At university, my wonderful mentor, Art Mother Glenys, found me and saw me through it all. She still does.

After Mum died, Dad continued to run the business. With drink and grief, he sunk into depression. He ruled with an iron fist. Strangely, we felt safe in the pub. As young girls working the bar after school and on weekends with alcohol and men (often very strange and drunk), we were never scared. We learned how to take charge of ourselves in public spaces.

Dad has had minor relationships with women, but

affected my older sister. When she reached the age Mum died, she had 'that forty-four fear.' I am not there yet.

I have had some unfortunate suitors. Until now. Rejection and abandonment, those old feelings of loss and self-worth, have been massive for me. I

The loneliness was huge. I remember the feelings, but not the details.

no real relationships after Mum. He never remarried. About five years ago we finally had it out and I told him it felt like he'd forgotten that he still had two young children to take care of when Mum died. He listened with his head in his hands as I ranted. I suddenly understood. He's not just my father, he's a man. He'd had his struggles with Mum's early death and he still does. Age has softened him.

I feel our mother's death really

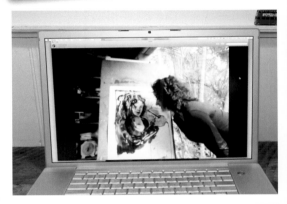

believe I explore aspects of this in a public way in my performance art by responding and remaining in the present.

I feel blessed to have the creative insight to be able to put all the situations I have coped with into the language of visual art. Maybe this has been the gift.

She never once spoke of *cancer or death.*

Me: 17 Mom: 56

Liz Shelley, USA

At eighteen I finished school a semester early, sold our house and drove by myself to be with my father. I remember feeling so abandoned and alone.

My mother died July 30, 1986.

The night she died was the night I returned to the hospital after purposefully staying away for three days. Her last words as she slipped in and out of consciousness were very hurtful to me, and I didn't know how to make sense of that so I avoided seeing her. Now I look back and realize she might have meant any number of things that were frustrating to her as she was dying.

My dad was on a cot in the corner and I sat in a chair by the bed, holding her hand and watching her. As her

I have learned that if you don't risk, you lose the opportunity

for growth and love.

breathing started to labour, I spoke quietly and told her I would be okay, and for her to go.

My mother was very stoic. During her battle with cancer she never once spoke of it, or of death.

After she died, if felt like everyone disappeared. My two older brothers lived on their own and far from me. My father had accepted a job that required him to move and was travelling back and forth while I stayed at home to finish high school. Because of these circumstances, we didn't grieve together as a family.

The plan was for my mother and me to live at home and join my father after graduation. Her death set us on a different path.

At seventeen I ended up by myself and lonely in the house with a grieving father who was only home twenty-five percent of the time. I felt a sense of

betrayal from his actions. All I wanted to know was, "why didn't you stay with me?"

As a teenager I did not understand the financial necessity of his new job, or the decisions and the actions made on my behalf. I had lost a mother, yet he had lost his spouse, as well as the person who could help manage me as a teenager. It felt like he was too scarred from her death to stay with me.

At eighteen I finished school a semester early, sold our house and drove by myself to be with my father. I remember feeling so abandoned and alone.

I was determined to succeed and I have. While I've struggled with my mother's death and its impact on me, I found the strength to finish college, and have been rewarded with a successful professional life.

I have come to terms with the fear and emotions resulting from the loss of my mother. I now know that my father did the best that he could too. Had my mother lived, I'm sure I would have been a different person, but personality comes from life's experiences. Losing my mother at a young age is part of my personality and what defines me now as an adult.

It's not easy for me to let people into my circle of trust. I became controlling over my emotions because I lost control of my life at a young age. I was afraid to take emotional risks. But I have learned that if you don't risk, you lose the opportunity for growth and love.

I have been called intimidating and told that I have a hard shell and walls of steel. In reality, under all of that, I want to love and be loved.

As a seventeen-year-old, the abandonment and fear I felt with the loss of my mother was crippling. As an adult, I understand that I've grown from it. It has given me true strength.

When you lose your mom,
it feels like an open wound.

Me: 19 Mom: 44

Carolyn Pritchard, Canada

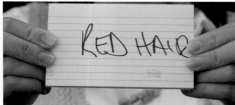

My early personal relationships were measured against unrealistic expectations. Maybe I was looking to fill a void and for someone to take away the sadness. I realize now how impossible it is to ask this of someone else.

It was September 28, 1989. Nobody ever asks you to talk about the day your mom died and that's really sad. Maybe a therapist might, but nobody that matters, like your friends or family.

I was seventeen and in high school when Mom got sick. We had home care and I remember that Dad would be in the driveway talking to the nurses, peppering them with questions for as long as he could keep them there: What was going to happen? Is she getting better?

Mom accepted the fate of her disease without treatment.

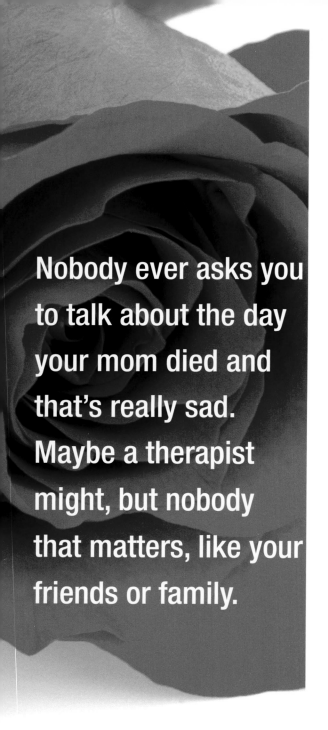

Nobody ever asks you to talk about the day your mom died and that's really sad. Maybe a therapist might, but nobody that matters, like your friends or family.

Dad supported her decision, but we were praying and hoping for a miracle.

I was in first-year nursing when she died. For the first while I tried to come home every weekend to see Dad because he was so sad and lonely. Because of this I didn't get a chance to really jell with people at school. I didn't have the university experience I had hoped for. On my weekend trips home, we would both share in the heartbreak my dad was living daily.

University was important to Mom. She didn't go. We grew up in a small town and she worked at our local public school as a receptionist before she went into real estate. I don't think she was ever content, and that's why she really pushed my sister and me to go, and we did. She wanted us to be educated and independent women.

After Mom died, we just went on living. Both my sister and I were away at school. Dad cleared out our family home and then moved about six or seven times to different towns. You could tell he had trouble with closure, even delaying getting her headstone for a couple of years. It was also very difficult for my sister and me to visit, as our sense of home was no longer.

Dad was lonely and he did date after Mom died. He went through a phase where people were setting him up, however he was not over my mom and was too sad to move on.

My early personal relationships were measured against unrealistic expectations. Maybe I was looking to fill a void and for someone to take away the sadness. I realize now how impossible it is to ask this of someone else.

When you lose your mom, it feels like an open wound. When you meet someone who's gone through it, there's an instant understanding, a shared journey, some general sense that you should talk.

Ironically, the one person I knew who did go through it was my mom. Maybe this was why she often seemed so sad. Only recently have I begun to understand what it might have been like for her to lose her mother so young too.

Afte twenty-one years, Dad has been blessed with another Joan to love. She's Joan Pritchard now, just like my mom. And she's lovely. I am grateful that she is so kind to my daughter.

It was a very cruel death
for a beautiful spirit.

Me: 29 Mom: 69

Margaret Alden, Canada

I don't think any of us can deny our experiences, even if we do lock them away. They still influence us.

Mom died on December 11, 1990. A severe stroke left her with brain damage and the inability to speak or eat on her own. It was devastating. She lived like that for eighteen months. After about a year in a rehabilitation centre Mom came home to live with Dad.

Mom was always a very proud woman and we thought she'd be embarrassed to see people, so Dad wouldn't let anyone but family see her. We kept up a rotation to look after her. At that time I was living a distance away, so I was driving back and forth a lot. I was newly married, pregnant and managing a high-stress job at the same time.

It shouldn't have been such a shock,

but it was a terrible shock.

I was in the bedroom when I got the phone call from my sister. It shouldn't have been a shock, but it was a terrible shock. It's funny because I look back and I hear myself crying and crying, but I don't actually see myself in my body.

My then-husband came in with our son, who was six months old at the time. He wanted me to take him because he thought it would stop the crying. It didn't. I was really, really devastated. My grief became very hard on our marriage. I cried so much that I got afraid to cry and even to this day, anytime I get sad it links back.

I don't think any of us can deny our experiences, even if we do lock them away. They still influence us.

My mother really was my best friend, so even when I lived away from home, we talked on the phone every single day. I felt abandoned for a long time.

In fact, when both kids went off to university, I had those old feelings of abandonment and I realize now that they were linked to losing Mom.

Mom was the matriarch of our family. We were lost without her. Our family was never the same afterward. She had unique relationships with each of us and so many special gifts.

Her generosity of spirit even showed up in the way she died. My parents sat after dinner with the cats, and my dad always slept with his head on my mom's lap at night, so they were still continuing that somehow. The cats were outside. Dad was asleep and she, in her fragile, fragile state, somehow got up and was trying to let them in when she fell and stroked and died.

It was a very cruel death for a beautiful spirit.

We were all worried about Dad

because he had never been alone before. Eventually he got involved with another lady. We were okay with it because it seemed to really give him new life.

I think we would have been fine if he'd decided to remarry. I don't know whether he said this or whether this was the sense I had, that he would never get married again because nobody could ever replace Mom.

I still feel like I'm a young person not to have a mom around. There are so many things I've confronted without my mom's wisdom, but I know I'm not alone. I've had many odd experiences where things have just about been tragic, but not. My father is gone now too, and at those moments I always think, "Thanks, Mom and Dad," because I don't know how else to explain them. I believe a lot in guardian angels and so I believe my parents are around. And I do feel their love.

I'm looking forward to
wrinkles and grey hair.

Me: 14 Mom: 48

Elizabeth Van Den Kerkhof, Canada

Afterward I don't ever remember crying with my dad. Maybe with my sisters a few times. We had to get up to speed fast with the new way of doing things. It was the SILENCE. I don't remember talking to anyone about it. Not even at school.

Mom was in the hospital but she had come home just before Christmas and I remember her worrying about how she would get gifts for everybody. She couldn't get out of bed.

It was January 24, 1975 and I was fourteen. We didn't know she was dying, but I have a feeling she knew. As I've grown older, I often wonder what it must have been like for her to have to leave seven children behind with the youngest just three. And Mom's sister in the Netherlands had died two weeks earlier at age thirty-seven from breast cancer. That must have been brutal.

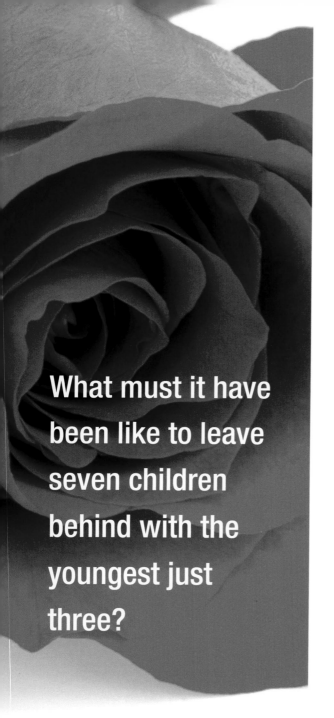

What must it have been like to leave seven children behind with the youngest just three?

Sometime before Christmas, Mom managed to get us to a store and she bought twenty pairs of underwear for each of us. Maybe she was thinking, "Oh my God, who is going to buy them underwear?" That's all I know about her preparation, but there must have been more to it.

Afterward I don't ever remember crying with my dad. Maybe with my sisters a few times. We had to get up to speed fast with the new way of doing things. It was the SILENCE. I don't remember talking to anybody about it. Not even at school.

Christmas became awful. As a young nurse, I would take all the Christmas shifts. My excuse to everyone was it was fine because I didn't have a family at home.

My mom did all the books for our dairy farm and helped

outside as well. After she died the place went to hell in a hand basket. Everything just stopped when Mom got sick. My dad was devoted to her too, and he spent almost every day in the hospital with her for a year.

Dad got interested in other women after she died and it caused all sorts of problems. Maybe he was looking for someone to care about his children. We had to run the farm on our own. Later we would chuckle and say, "Mom died and dad went AWOL." We would become close in weathering the storms ahead.

My oldest brother, John, committed suicide when he was thirty-seven. I do think that this was a direct result of Mom's death. He was twenty-one when she died. He'd been a rebellious teenager and he often fought with her. I remember well his feelings of guilt after she died.

You try not to let trauma define you, but I think it does. Especially if you're young. If she hadn't died young would I still have been someone looking over my shoulder, focused on trying to stay ahead of what might happen next? Safety and security are huge for me and so is independence.

I didn't get married until I was thirty-three. I was waiting for a guy that would "get" me. I didn't think I could put myself in that vulnerable spot again. I didn't want to put children through it and I didn't want to go back and do it again, losing a child, for example.

Now I'm past the age my mother was when she died and my son is older than I was when she died too. So far, so good. Many I know fear getting old, but I'm looking forward to wrinkles and grey hair because that will mean I'll have lived long enough to have them.

If I die young, will my kids remember me doing things like braiding my daughter's hair, cooking my son's hot chocolate? I'll do anything for them, give them any experience, take them anywhere.

That's the lesson I take away from this: Invest in your family.

It was over fifty years ago, but I can still feel the pain.

Me: 26 Mom: 52
Shirley Anne (Towriss) Ross, Canada

The fact that my mother was killed in a car accident is never, ever out of my mind. I think, what if we get in a car accident? What would that mean for my children?

I remember the knock at the door and the two policemen standing there.

Mom and Dad were in a neighbour's car and the car hit the shoulder and rolled. My mother was killed instantly. Dad was in the back seat and he was very badly injured. In fact, they took him to a nearby hospital to die, but he fooled them.

I was seven months pregnant with my second child, Mary-Ellen. Our first born, Tim, was almost two and my younger daughter, Laurie, was yet to be. Tim was with

People said that time heals everything.

I just didn't want to hear that stuff.

me. We had been planning a picnic that day.

I guess I called someone to go and get my husband, Lloyd, from the golf course. From then on that day is a blur.

It was over fifty years ago but I can still feel the pain. I am an only child. My mother and I were very close. She was really my mentor.

I remember the months afterward vividly. My dad had a funeral business and someone had to carry it on while he was in the hospital, so we moved from Owen Sound to Arthur, Ontario to look after Dad and the business.

I had no real friends there and no one to talk with about my mother's death. Except for my husband. He's always been my rock. After that it was Lloyd and I against the world.

I can remember going uptown to get groceries. I'd work my way up to the store with people stopping me and trying to be kind and saying things like "time heals everything." I just didn't want to hear that stuff.

We stayed in Arthur with Dad for two years, but then finally I couldn't handle it anymore and so he hired a young couple to run the business and we moved back so that Lloyd could go back to his old job.

My dad had a massive heart attack after Mom died. He remarried, but that didn't last because he had a drinking problem and he was a smoker. I loved my stepmother. I thought she was very sweet and I didn't blame her for leaving at all. When she left, we never heard from her again. Everybody would say, "she'll be back, she'll be back," but then Dad died. She was very different from my mother, but she was a lovely person.

The fact that my mother was killed in a car accident is never, ever out of my mind. I think, what if we get in a car accident? What would that mean for my children?

The day it happened, Mom was going to a picnic. And they were with a couple that they never, ever socialized with. That bothered me. My mother shouldn't have been there in the first place. I felt very angry and very, very bitter at the woman who was driving. Of course I know it wasn't her fault. I've tried not to think that, but I've got to admit that it still rankles.

I have no closure. And it doesn't seem to matter how many years have gone by.

Photos submitted by Shirley Anne (Town...

After my mother died, everything changed.
She was the heart of the family.

Me: 19 Mom: 54

Gwen Osborne, Canada

Soon after Mother's death, I took sick. I think it was a nervous breakdown, really, because of the shock of having my mother taken away from me so quickly.

It was October 6, 1941.

I remember it was a lovely day and we were expecting her home from the hospital. Mother had been rushed there in the middle of the night with a heart attack she'd taken a couple of days earlier. That was all we knew. We thought she was getting better, but then word came that she was dead. And that was that. We didn't go to doctors back then, so if she had a condition, she wasn't aware of it. She'd had ten children. That might have weakened her.

One of my sisters had married very young and she, her husband and their three children lived with us. That day was their oldest daughter's birthday, and even though Mother had just died, the little girl insisted on having her birthday party that day. That was very unsettling.

My father had a very busy life as a contractor and I remember that the funeral parlour was just crowded with people, flowers, gifts.

Dad was too busy to be at home much, but I did have very close friends and they rallied around me. Soon after Mother's death, I took sick. I think it was a nervous break-down, really, because of the shock of having my mother taken away from me so quickly.

I worked very hard to pull myself together and go back and complete high school. I also took a business course.

My husband and I have four children and they were always busy. I did lots of volunteer work when I could. We moved a lot with a young family and everyone needed me home. Besides, my delight has always been my children.

After my mother died, everything changed. She was the heart of the family. We had a very big void because Mother was someone who attended to things. She wasn't bossy, she just saw that things were done. And we always seemed to have relatives visiting or staying with us. We always had about twenty or twenty-five people for supper on Sunday and we didn't after that.

I felt more on my own, responsible for myself, after she was gone. I wasn't lonely because there was always

somebody around. I think that I was just determined to be on my own and to get along in my own life.

I've never really considered what happened from a man's point of view, but I'm sure my father missed Mother very much because she was always

For some reason I've never worried about dying young. I had a sister die at forty-two, another at fifty, another at fifty-four and a brother at fifty-four.

I know I missed my mother very much when she died. Dad was there if I asked him for something, but I didn't want to

It does change over the years. I will never forget her but the pain softens with time.

there for him. He was a hunter and he used to spend a lot of time away in the fall, but he was always good with the family.

My father did meet a lady that owned the fishing camp where he went often and he got very involved in going there later in his life. But he never remarried. He died in his own home and this woman, Elizabeth, looked after him for at least twenty years, so I don't have any hard feelings towards her.

ask him for anything. I always wanted to do it on my own and I still do. I think this part of my personality came about because of losing my mother so young.

It does change over the years. I will never forget her but the pain softens with time.

My mother was sunshine and energy.
Our home was always full of laughter.

Me: 23 Mom: 49

Linda Gayle Ross, Canada

I felt like I had lost my best friend. It would be years before I could safely explore the "Mom" section of any card store without tears.

Mom died at 5:03 p.m. on an strangely warm Saskatchewan winter day. She had been sick for about five years but, as always, she remained high spirited and good natured. I don't know if she was afraid, because we never talked about it. I do know that we did not believe she would die.

Eventually her breast cancer was everywhere.

My mother came from a mystical Scottish family and she had grown up with spiritual practices that were some-times at odds with my father's traditional family back-

ground. Some of those early practices I recall as a kid are now almost mainstream. Her family name was Patience, and it would turn out that patience was one of her most needed personality traits in dealing with my dad.

She was also hardworking, gentle and generous. We owned a prosperous Saskatchewan grain farm and there were many helpers to house and feed, in addition to others in need who often stayed with us or at our table, all under my mother's wing.

We spent late fall and winter in our home in the nearby city. As Mom was getting sicker, Dad started either buying or investing in local small businesses, and there was lots of entertaining happening. By then my mother was coming to the end of her life, while my father was sowing the seeds of the alcoholism that would rule

much of the remainder of his.

After the funeral, my pregnant older sister returned home to Manitoba with her husband and six-month-old son. The shock of Mom's death was so great for her that she ended up on bed rest for the remainder of that pregnancy.

I felt abandoned and I was really angry with my father who, in my view, had stolen her last few years with his increased drinking.

I felt like I had lost my best friend. It would be years before I could safely explore the "Mom" section of any card store without tears.

After Mom died, Dad turned all of her photos upside down, hid them in his dresser drawer and started drinking even more heavily. He could not say her name, Dora, for years. He hated being on the land without her. We all missed her so much. Without consultation, he sold our family farm and he never worked again.

Dad was now handsome, charming and very eligible. For the next twenty-five years, women came and went from his life amid bouts of binge drinking and drama. All the while, my sister and I cleaned up the messes he got himself into with the various women who vied to be Wife Number Two.

Finally, at the age of 82, Dad sunk into a clinical depression. My sister and I rescued him — again. I brought him to my home city and we launched into a three-year caregiving odyssey. We helped him out of his life and despite the many challenges, it was a fabulous gift that the three of us shared.

I feel like I've been a wanderer for a lot of my adult life. I was seeking a safe place. I now understand that you cannot find a safe place, you must create one for yourself. I've lived in five Canadian provinces and the USA. Along the way, I made sure to get a solid education. I have been married more than once. I regret that some of my decisions have caused unhappiness for others.

In so many ways my father was a great guy. I have forgiven him my broken heart. I hope that he has forgiven me my mistakes as his daughter.

I am grateful for my family — husband, daughter, son-in-law, stepchildren, grandchildren.

From my first marriage came my daughter, Dorie. She is my heartbeat. It still stings when she refers to my mother as "your mom." Not because of the words or any insensitivity on her part. It's simply that Dora and Dorie never met.

Lessons

What do we make of this experience of early mother loss?

Is it the events or the decisions that we make about the events in our lives that matter? As Eleanor Roosevelt reminds us, "in the long run, we shape our lives and we shape ourselves."

We want to believe that there's a reason for loss, for tragic events. But what if it just happened— an accident, a sudden illness, killer cancer? And the result is that a young girl becomes self-reliant and independent, or too dependent, or too cautious about trusting, or not cautious at all. How do we understand these responses?

Are they decisions or are they just what happened?

Losing a mother young leaves its legacy — abandonment, denial, loneliness, silence, shame — instincts that may last a lifetime. We are no longer our mother's daughter.

The lifetime journey ahead will warrant countless stops without her, each one a sharp reminder of what we've lost.

Mothers are supposed to always be there. As much as we try, we cannot control how we feel or what we think. For some, grief becomes a constant companion. As American surgeon and psychiatrist Gordon Livingston points out, "to lose that which has meant everything to us is a lesson in helplessness, humility and survival. There is no way around it, you have to go through it."

As we go through it, and continue The Journey, we must take care not to let nostalgia for our perfect mother, an idealized past, a spotless family, disguise our attempts to come to terms with the present, the new regime, our future.

The Girls in the Front Row are living the lessons learned in humility, the power of chance and the courage needed to triumph. We are opening our hearts again, the biggest risk of all.

Reach out. Ask for help, accept it. Forgive. Take risks. Let others in. Invest in your family and your friends. Help someone else. Don't bottle up grief; it will break and scatter. Talk, talk, talk to someone who will listen patiently, respectfully. Keep talking until it feels like there's nothing left to say. Create, make something, record and keep your special memories safe. These memories will make you stronger, more generous, wiser, kinder.

It will get better.

80

The Girls in the Front Row

81

The Girls in the Front Row

P.S. Dear Dads

We need you to be our hero.

Choose us first. Before yourself and before your next love. It's not forever, just while we learn to breathe without her.

Someone else, too soon, may interrupt our grief. And yours. If this happens it may be years, if ever, before we get back on track. Time, patience and grit will help us both journey well.

Our challenge is to learn to trust again, to feel safe and hopeful. We'll take our cue from you regarding moral behaviours, obligations, responsibilities. If your words do not match your behaviour, we'll focus on your behaviour. We've already learned that behaviour is the only form of communication we can count on.

As we grow older we'll understand more of your loss, your fatigue, your fears — how grief and loneliness can influence decisions.

Now we need your firm direction and support, even as we resist your attempts to help, your rules, regulations and the new order, life without Mom. Don't give up on us. We must learn and earn true independence by following your example. Along the way our grief may stretch your emotional and financial resources.

We thank you. In time we will be grateful.

We need at least one person we can rely on, share our feelings with, trust to not run away. If you can't be this person, help us find someone who can — a close relative, our Aunt Matilda, a compassionate counsellor. Our mother's death may change everything we believe in, our faith framework.

We must keep some of her things, to remind us of her essence and to help us recall her love in the years to come. We may need a special school, a safe and supportive learning environment, kind spaces filled with even just a few wise hearts.

Most of all, we need to know we're still lovable, still loved. Help us believe this by letting our needs rise above your own now. If you can do this, we'll have the best opportunity possible to play the cards we've been dealt with acceptance and grace.

A friend says that it's easy to spot a motherless daughter because she has not been "sufficiently kissed." As Front Row Girls, help us choose the right ways to get sufficiently kissed in life.

We need your clear head and broad shoulders. In time we'll reward you with respect, devotion and a bouquet of red roses in bloom.

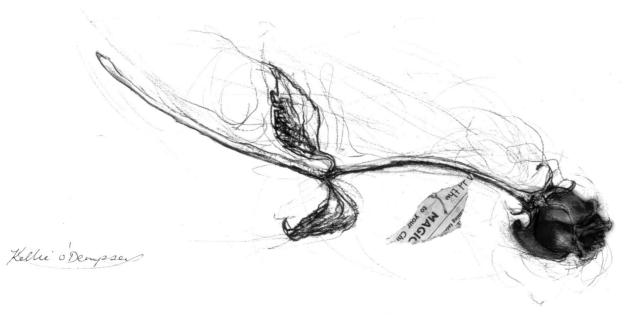

Kellie O'Dempsey

Selected Reading

Edelson, Hope. *Motherless Daughters: The Legacy of Loss* (Second Edition). Harper. New York. 2006.

Moore, Thomas. *Dark Nights of the Soul: A Guide to Finding Your Way Through Life's Ordeals.* Gotham. New York. 2005.